LIVING GREEN

Forests and Wetlands

a Scott Fetzer company

Chicago

www.worldbookonline.com

Editorial:

Editor in Chief: Paul A. Kobasa
Project Manager: Cassie Mayer
Writer: Al Smuskiewicz
Editor: Daniel Kenis
Researchers: Daniel Kenis, Jacqueline Jasek
Manager, Contracts & Compliance
 (Rights & Permissions): Loranne K. Shields
Indexer: David Pofelski

Graphics and Design:

Associate Director: Sandra M. Dyrlund
Manager: Tom Evans
Coordinator, Design Development
 and Production: Brenda B. Tropinski
Book design by: Don Di Sante
Designer: Matthew Carrington
Contributing Photographs Editor: Clover Morell
Senior Cartographer: John Rejba

Pre-Press and Manufacturing:

Director: Carma Fazio
Manufacturing Manager: Steve Hueppchen
Production/Technology Manager: Anne Fritzinger

World Book, Inc.
233 N. Michigan Avenue
Chicago, IL 60601
U.S.A.

For information about other World Book publications, visit
our Web site at **http://www.worldbookonline.com** or call
1-800-WORLDBK (967-5325).
For information about sales to schools and libraries, call
1-800-975-3250 (United States), or **1-800-837-5365 (Canada)**.

Library of Congress Cataloging-in-Publication Data

Forests and wetlands.
    p. cm. -- (Living green)
   Includes index.
   Summary: "General overview of forest and wetland ecosystems, including an
exploration of disturbances these ecosystems face due to human interference
and climate change, and current conservation and reclamation efforts. Features
include fact boxes, sidebars, activities, glossary, list of recommended reading and
Web sites, and index"--Provided by publisher.
   ISBN 978-0-7166-1401-2
   1. Forests and forestry--Juvenile literature. 2. Forest ecology--Juvenile
literature. 3. Wetlands--Juvenile literature. I. World Book, Inc.
QH86.F6596 2009
577.3—dc22
                                  2008024117

Picture Acknowledgments:

Front Cover: © Phil Degginger, Alamy Images

© Niall Benvie, Alamy Images 21; © Custom Life
Science Images/Alamy Images 48; © Moodboard/
Alamy Images 7; © Nic Miller, Organics Image
Library/Alamy Images 1; © Edward Parker, Alamy
Images 32; © C.C. Lockwood, Animals Animals
30; AP/Wide World 29, 36, 37, 50, 55; © Adrian
Arbib from Peter Arnold Inc. 35; © Biosphoto/
Peter Arnold Inc. 10, 20, 25, 26, 28; © David
Cavagnaro from Peter Arnold Inc. 16; © Mark
Edwards from Peter Arnold Inc. 52; © Ricardo
Funari from Peter Arnold Inc. 33; © R. Frank from
Peter Arnold Inc. 19; © Jeff Greenberg from Peter
Arnold Inc. 44; © Alan Majchrowicz from Peter
Arnold Inc. 12; © J. Mallwitz from Peter Arnold
Inc. 39; © L.C. Marigo from Peter Arnold Inc. 8;
© Juan Pablo Moreiras from Peter Arnold Inc. 40;
© Tom Murphy from Peter Arnold, Inc. 17; © P.
Oxford from Peter Arnold Inc. 24; © Ed Reschke
from Peter Arnold Inc. 6, 9; © Johann
Schumacher from Peter Arnold Inc. 42;
© Wildlife/Peter Arnold Inc. 13; © AFP/Getty
Images 57; © Altrendo Nature/Getty Images 49;
© Tim Fitzharris, Getty Images 18; © Michael &
Patricia Fogden, Getty Images 22; © Image Bank/
Getty Images 51; © Larry Minden, Getty Images 17;
© Oxford Scientific Photolibrary/Getty Images 34;
© Photodisc/Getty Images 47; © Time & Life
Pictures/Getty Images 54; © Kirk Weddle, Getty
Images 46; © Norbert Wu, Getty Images 14;
NASA/Earth Observatory 56; © Shutterstock 4, 5,
13, 25, 29, 31, 41, 42, 45, 46.

All maps and illustrations are the exclusive
property of World Book, Inc.

Living Green
Set ISBN: 978-0-7166-1400-5
Printed in China
2 3 4 5 6 13 12 11 10 09

Table of Contents

Introduction 4

What Are Forests? 6

Forest Ecology 8

Temperate Deciduous Forests 10

Temperate Coniferous Forests .14

Boreal Forests 18

Tropical Rain Forests 22

Tropical Seasonal Forests 26

Logging 30

Farming 32

Industrial Pollution 34

Warfare 36

Climate Change 38

What Are Wetlands? 40

Wetland Ecology 42

Marshes 44

Swamps 46

Bogs and Fens 48

Human Settlement 50

Pollution 52

Invasive Species 54

Climate Change 56

Activities 58

Glossary 60

Additional Resources 62

Index 63

Some words in the text appear in bold, **like this.** They are defined in the glossary on pages 60-61. Words are bolded at the first use in each section.

Introduction

Section Summary

Forests provide us with such resources as wood, medicines, and food. They also create the oxygen we breathe, and they help regulate Earth's weather and climate.

Like forests, wetlands perform many benefits for humans and the environment. They clean wastes from water, prevent floods, and provide food.

Today, forests and wetlands face a number of threats caused by human activities.

Sunlight filters through the foliage of a thick forest canopy.

Forests and wetlands easily capture our imagination. Throughout history, these wild places have given rise to many fascinating myths and legends. Folklore is filled with stories about such magical creatures as unicorns, elves, and fairies living in enchanted forests. Wetland areas, such as swamps and bogs, have been said to be lurking with such frightening beings as bogeymen, werewolves, and zombies.

These tales can amaze us, delight us, or frighten us. However, the reality of forests and wetlands can be just as wonderful as the stories. The great diversity of living things found in these real-world environments rivals the mythological beasts encountered in novels and movies.

Features of forests and wetlands

Forests are found throughout the world, from hot, rainy regions to cold, dry regions. Different areas have their own special kinds of forests. In some areas, forests are packed with trees and shrubs that grow so lushly that little sunlight can shine through the **foliage** to reach the forest floor. Giant spiders and snakes quietly move about in the shade, while chattering monkeys and multicolored birds make noise high in the sunny branches. In other areas, forests grow with majestic trees that are taller than the Statue of Liberty and older than Columbus's voyages to America. Forests are home to such fierce predators (hunters) as wolves, tigers, cougars, and owls, as well as such plant eaters as deer, elephants, sloths, and sparrows.

Marshes, swamps, bogs, and other wetlands are also found in many places around the world. Some of these wetlands have surfaces that resemble spongy trampolines. People can even walk and jump on the surfaces, making the plants in the area shake up and down. Other wetlands have strange trees with knobby "knees" that stick out of the water to "breathe" in air. Some plants in wetlands act like predatory animals, capturing and digesting insects. Alligators, crocodiles, and snapping turtles are some of the large predators that inhabit wetlands. Waterfowl—swimming birds, such as ducks and geese—and wading birds—long-legged birds, such as herons and egrets—are so abundant in some wetlands that they can completely cover the water surface.

Wetlands have soil that remains water-logged for most of the year.

Importance of forests and wetlands

Forests provide us with food, oxygen, wood, paper, and medicines. They also help **regulate** Earth's weather and climate (weather patterns over long periods). Wetlands perform many beneficial actions for us—including cleaning wastes from water, preventing floods, and providing us with fish, shellfish, and other food.

Today, forests and wetlands face a number of threats caused by human activities. Among these threats are pollution, destruction of **habitats**, and climate change. Fortunately, we can all work together to help ensure the survival of forests and wetlands—and all the amazing creatures and stories they contain.

What Are Forests?

Section Summary

There are many types of forests, each with particular kinds of trees, other plants, and animals.

Forest ecosystems are changing due to such human activities as logging and the clearing of land for agriculture and development. Pollution from vehicles, factories, and power plants also damages forests.

Scientists are already seeing the effects of global warming on forests. Disease-carrying germs and insects are becoming more common. They cause significant damage to forest habitats.

Evergreen forests grow along the edge of the tundra in Alaska.

A forest is a place that can overwhelm the senses. Trees tower into the sky all around. Their leaves and trunks come in many colors, textures, shapes, and sizes. Leaves form a ceiling above, rustling in the wind and filtering the sunlight as it shines down through the **foliage** to the soil.

Smaller plants lie between the trees, such as thorny shrubs and fragrant wildflowers. Some of the shrubs have brightly colored fruits on their twigs. The sounds of singing birds, chirping chipmunks, and buzzing insects fill the air. There are also signs of other animals, such as teeth marks on the trunk of a tree (left by a beaver) and a hole in the ground (dug by a fox). Smells fill the air, too—perhaps even the unpleasant odor left by a skunk.

Forests form one of the major kinds of **biomes** in nature. A biome is a community of plants and animals covering a widespread region with special characteristics. The main feature of a forest is its trees. Forests contain trees of different species (kinds), sizes, and ages growing close together. They also have woody shrubs and soft-stemmed herbs between the trees. In addition, many species of fungi, insects, worms, amphibians, reptiles, birds, mammals, and other organisms live in forests, too. Taken together, a forest's soil, trees, and all the other plants, animals, and living things form an important **ecosystem** (a community of interconnected living and nonliving elements of a natural area).

Types of forests

There are different types of forests, each with particular kinds of trees, other plants, and animals. The makeup of any forest depends on a number of factors, such as the temperatures and amount of **precipitation** in a region. A forest's trees may be evergreen—that is, their leaves stay green all year. Or they may be **deciduous**—that is, their leaves fall off at a certain time of year.

Evergreen needleleaf trees, such as fir and spruce, are common in forests in cold northern regions, such as Canada. Deciduous broadleaf trees, such as oak and hickory, are common in warmer regions farther south, such as the eastern United States. Evergreen broadleaf trees, such as palms and mahogany trees, grow in forests in hot, rainy tropical regions.

The animal life of forests also varies from place to place. There are bears and beavers in northern forests and monkeys and macaws in tropical forests.

Importance of forests

Forests are important not only as wildlife **habitats**, but also as places with useful resources for people. Lumber, plywood, paper, and cardboard are made from trees. Fuel used for cooking and heating, as well as fats, oils, and gums used in manufacturing, are obtained from trees. Many medicines for treating people with cancer, heart disease, and other illnesses are derived from plants and animals found in forests.

Forests also have values that go beyond such practical uses. Many people enjoy forests for such recreational activities as camping, hiking, bird watching, fishing, and hunting. The wild environment of a forest can be a source of beauty and wonder.

Forests are an important habitat for many unique plants and animals, such as these young owls.

FOREST ECOLOGY

A look inside a forest reveals a complex community of plants and animals, from tiny mosses to mighty oaks, and from small insects to huge elk. However, a forest contains even more than meets the eye. Many microscopic and underground organisms are also part of the forest ecosystem.

The forest food chain

In a forest ecosystem, energy flows through interconnected **food chains** from plants to animals and back to plants. This flow forms a cycle involving many **producers** (plants and algae), **consumers** (animals), and **decomposers** (bacteria and fungi).

Forests support many living things. This red howler monkey eats leaves from a tree in the Amazon rain forest.

Trees, shrubs, and other plants are the primary producers. These organisms have **chloroplasts**, tiny green "factories" in their cells. A process called **photosynthesis** takes place inside these chloroplasts. In this process, a substance called chlorophyll makes food for the plant by using the energy of sunlight to chemically combine water from soil with the gas **carbon dioxide** from air. The plants release oxygen into the air as a **by-product** of photosynthesis.

Consumers can be divided into different levels, depending on how far removed their food is from the forest plants. **Herbivores** (plant-eating animals) are the forest's primary, or first-level, consumers. These animals, such as caterpillars, eat leaves or other parts of plants to obtain energy to live. Various **carnivores** (animals that eat other animals) and **omnivores** (animals that eat both plants and other animals) are the secondary consumers. They may eat plants, or they may eat the primary consumers. For example, shrews eat the caterpillars. The top predators in a forest ecosystem, such as owls, are known as the tertiary, or third-level, consumers. They eat the secondary consumers.

Decomposers, such as bacteria and fungi in the soil, break down the dead bodies of all producers and consumers. The process of **decomposition** returns nutrients and minerals to the soil, where plants use them to fuel their growth.

Succession of forests

The forest you see today may have been a farm field 200 or 300 years ago. When farmland is abandoned, nature can take over. Winds and animals carry seeds of plants to the area. First, grasses, herbs, and shrubs sprout on the land, forming a meadow. As decades pass, more and more trees take root. Eventually, if conditions are right, the site becomes a full-grown forest with a dense growth of trees. This process of development is called **ecological succession.**

An old growth forest—a forest that has been growing for many hundreds of years—is a healthy, complex ecosystem. It contains living trees of many species, sizes, and ages, as well as fallen logs and large, standing dead trees, called snags. Many birds, mammals, and other animals have habitats in old growth forests.

A healthy forest is beneficial to people. Forest plants and soils absorb water from rain and snowmelt, reducing flooding in nearby towns and cities. As this water filters through the forest, plant roots and soil capture some chemicals that would otherwise pollute **ground water** supplies used by people. Forest predators, such as hawks and owls, eat rats and other animal pests. Some bees and other insects that pollinate crops and garden plants come from forests.

Old growth forests are complex ecosystems with a large variety of trees and animals.

TEMPERATE DECIDUOUS FORESTS

Temperate deciduous forests are familiar to many people in the United States. The word *temperate* refers to a climate that is moderate in average temperature—not too cold (as in polar regions) or too hot (as in tropical regions). Temperate deciduous forests are found in much of eastern North America, east of the grasslands of the Great Plains and south of the boreal forests of Canada. Temperate deciduous forests are also found in western Europe and eastern Asia, including China, North and South Korea, and Japan. In the Southern Hemisphere, temperate deciduous forests grow on the southern tip of South America and in southeastern Australia and New Zealand.

Climate

Temperate deciduous forests grow in regions where summers are warm and winters are cold. The average summer temperature is approximately 68 °F (20 °C), while the average winter temperature is about 23 °F (−5 °C). During the year, the temperature may range widely, from greater than 90 °F (32 °C) to less than −20 °F (−29 °C). Harsh winter frosts are common in temperate deciduous forests.

Precipitation in a temperate deciduous forest is spread fairly evenly throughout the year. On average, between 28 and 60 inches (71 and 152 centimeters) of precipitation fall every year. Compared with other kinds of forests, this is a moderate amount of rainfall—more than boreal forests but not as much as rain forests. Some temperate deciduous forests are wetter than others. Regional differences in rainfall, temperature, and other factors result in different species of trees growing in the forests.

Life in temperate deciduous forests

Plants and animals in temperate deciduous forests experience all four seasons, with weather usually changing drastically from one season to the next—and sometimes from one week to the next. Temperate deciduous forests may experience frequent storms in spring and summer, including sudden tornadoes. In some forests that have survived severe tornadoes, groups of trees show permanent evidence of the strong winds by leaning and growing at an angle. The ability to survive such harsh weather is a type of **adaptation**—a physical or behavioral trait that helps an organism survive in its natural environment.

The growing season in regions with temperate deciduous forests lasts approximately half the year. Some plants, such as skunk cabbage, may begin growing as early as February. Skunk cabbage generates its own heat, allowing it to melt through snow cover. However, most plants in these forests grow from around April through September.

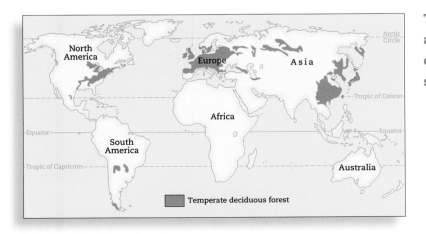

Temperate deciduous forests are moist forests that have cold winters and warm summers.

The leaves of maple trees become tinted with brilliant yellow, orange, and red colors in autumn.

Falling leaves

Most trees in temperate deciduous forests are deciduous broadleaf trees, which drop their leaves in autumn. Many people enjoy the red, orange, and yellow tints that the leaves take on before they fall. These colors are revealed when chlorophyll, the green pigment inside chloroplasts, breaks down. Tree leaves actually have a number of different colored pigments, and when chlorophyll disappears, these other pigments in the leaves can be seen.

Losing their leaves is an adaptation that allows the trees to preserve energy and survive winter **dormancy.** During winter, the trees do not grow or carry out photosynthesis. They resume growth and photosynthesis in spring, with the budding of fresh leaves.

The decay of fallen leaves adds many nutrients to the soil of temperate deciduous forests. This rich soil supports the growth of a wide variety of plants, as well as such fungi as mushrooms and bracket fungi.

Plant life

In most temperate deciduous forests, two or more species of trees dominate the landscape. For example, in moist areas of Indiana and Ohio, elm, maple, and beech trees are the dominant species. In drier areas of Illinois, Kentucky, and Tennessee, oak and hickory trees dominate the forests.

Many other tree species grow between dominant trees. Other common broadleaf trees in temperate deciduous forests include basswood, black cherry, walnut, and yellow poplar (also called the tulip tree). Most of these trees grow to heights between 60 and 100 feet (18 and 30 meters). Scattered coniferous (cone-bearing) trees, such as fir, pine, and spruce, may also be found, especially in areas with sandy soils.

Beneath these tall trees are many smaller trees, such as dogwood, redbud, and serviceberry. Beneath these, there is a layer of shrubs, including azalea, huckleberry, and rhododendron. At

Lynxes are forest predators.

ground level, herbs sprout every spring before the growth of tree leaves reduces the amount of sunlight reaching the forest floor. These herbs include such wildflowers as bloodroot, mayapple, and trillium.

Animal life

Animals in temperate deciduous forests include many insects, such as ants, beetles, and butterflies. Other small **invertebrates** (animals without backbones) are sow bugs, spiders, and worms. Amphibians include spring peeper frogs, chorus frogs, and tiger salamanders, while box turtles and fox snakes are some of the reptiles found in these forests.

Birds living year-round in temperate deciduous forests include blue jays, cardinals, chickadees, and crows. **Raptors** common in these forests include red-tailed hawks and great horned owls. In spring, many songbirds undertake long migrations (movements from one region to another with a change in season) to temperate deciduous forests from their winter homes farther south. These birds include warblers, wrens, tanagers, and thrushes.

Herbivores in temperate deciduous forests include beavers, chipmunks, gray squirrels, woodchucks, and white-tailed deer. Raccoons, opossums, skunks, red fox, and black bears are some omnivorous mammals in these forests. Large carnivores, such as cougars and wolves, are rare in most temperate deciduous forests because of centuries of trapping and hunting.

A CLOSER LOOK
Hibernation

Some animals in temperate deciduous forests hibernate through winter, meaning that their body temperature and heart rate drop dramatically while they sleep. For example, when a woodchuck goes into hibernation, its body temperature drops from about 98 °F to 38 °F (37 °C to 3°C), and its heart rate slows from about 80 beats per minute to 4 beats per minute.

Animals hibernate to protect themselves from the cold and to reduce their need for food, which is scarce in winter. During hibernation, animals live off their body fat.

A dormouse hibernates in a woodpecker's hole.

A temperate coniferous forest rises between a field and distant mountains in Jasper National Park, Canada.

TEMPERATE CONIFEROUS FORESTS

Walking in winter through a quiet forest filled with snow-covered evergreen trees can seem like a magical experience. Such forests are temperate coniferous forests. Most of the trees in these forests are **conifers**, which produce cones instead of flowers for reproduction. The trees' seeds develop inside the hard, woody cones.

Types of temperate coniferous forests

There are various types of temperate coniferous forests, each found in a different region with a somewhat different climate. A type of temperate coniferous forest known as a temperate rain forest occurs along seacoasts, including the Pacific Coast of North America from northern California to Canada and Alaska. Like tropical rain forests, temperate rain forests have abundant rainfall. North America's Pacific Northwest is home to the world's largest expanse of temperate rain forest. Smaller temperate rain forests are found near the sea in Norway, Scotland, southwestern South America, Australia, New Zealand, and Japan.

Another type of temperate coniferous forest, called montane forest, grows on low mountain slopes. Montane forests are found along the Rocky Mountains and the Sierra Nevada mountain range of western North America. They are also found in parts of Europe and Asia.

Still another type of temperate coniferous forest, sometimes referred to as mixed deciduous-evergreen forest, is found in the southeastern United States. These forests grow along the Atlantic Coast from Florida to Texas.

Climate

In general, the climate in regions with temperate coniferous forests is mild and moist. In northern coastal regions, the climate remains mild because the ocean retains heat better than the land. The temperatures in the ocean change very slowly, allowing the sea to keep its heat in winter, when the land loses its heat. Breezes blowing over the ocean are warmed by this heat and carry the warmth over the land. Thus, these warm breezes help prevent winters in northern coastal regions from becoming excessively cold. The opposite effect happens in summer, preventing summers from becoming very hot. In the temperate rain forests of the Pacific Northwest, temperatures rarely get below freezing or above 80 °F (27 °C).

Temperate rain forests—as their name implies—receive a great deal of rain and snow. Between 70 and 200 inches (178 and 508 centimeters) of precipitation fall in these forests each year. However, this is not as much rain as some tropical rain forests receive.

Montane forests have mild winters, though they have drier weather than temperate rain forests. In the mixed decidu-ous-evergreen forests of the southeastern United States, winter weather is usually mild and lasts for only a short time, but summers can be quite hot.

Temperate coniferous forests are found in Australia and areas of North and South America.

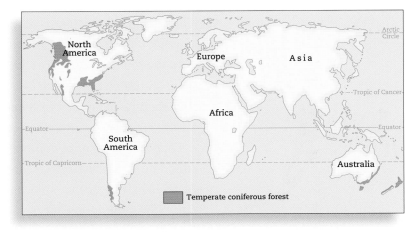

North America

Europe

Asia

Arctic Circle

Tropic of Cancer

Africa

Equator

Equator

South America

Tropic of Capricorn

Australia

Temperate coniferous forest

White fir trees grow thickly in this temperate coniferous forest in Trinity Alps, California.

Plant life

Scientists estimate that there is more biomass (amount of living biological material) in temperate rain forests than in any other kind of biome—approximately 500 tons per acre (1,120 metric tons per hectare). This is mainly because the largest trees in the world grow in these kinds of forests. Giant redwoods and sequoias are conifers that can soar to heights of more than 310 feet (94 meters), which is taller than the Statue of Liberty.

Other large conifers in these forests include Douglas fir, Sitka spruce, western hemlock, red cedar, and yellow cedar. Broadleaf trees mixed in with these conifers may include alders, cottonwoods, maples, and paper birch.

Many of the trees in temperate rain forests are covered with mosses and vines. Such plants are called **epiphytes** (*EHP uh fyts*)—that is, plants that grow on other plants for support but make their own food through photosynthesis. Epiphytes are different from parasites because they do not normally harm the trees on which they grow.

An assortment of shrubs with wild berries, such as huckleberry and salmonberry, are common in temperate rain forests. The forest floor is typically covered with a lush growth of ferns, mosses, lichens, and mushrooms.

In the montane forests of the lower slopes of the Rocky Mountains, pure stands of ponderosa pines make up much of the tree life. Slightly higher up the slopes, Douglas fir, white fir, and blue spruce are mixed with the pines.

Long-leaf pines once dominated the sandy coastal plains of the mixed deciduous-evergreen forests in the southeastern United States. These trees can survive forest fires, which once occurred naturally in the area. However, the suppression of forest fires by people has allowed many broadleaf trees to establish themselves in the pine forests.

Animal life

Wild animals living in temperate coniferous forests of western North America include several kinds of salamanders, frogs, toads, turtles, and snakes. The Pacific giant salamander, found in forests in this region, can grow to a length of more than 12 inches (30 centimeters). Birds that nest high in the tall conifers of temperate coniferous forests include the gray jay, pileated woodpecker, goshawk, and spotted owl. A number of seabirds, such as the marbled murrelet, are seen in these forests.

Small mammals living in western U.S. temperate coniferous forests include voles, marmots, martens, bats, and flying squirrels. Large mammals include black and brown bears, black-tailed deer, and elk. The cougar (also called mountain lion) is one of the more common large predators in parts of western temperate coniferous forests.

Animals of temperate coniferous forests include the Pacific giant salamander (left) and the pine marten (right).

GREEN FACT

The world's largest tree (as measured in volume of wood) is a giant sequoia in California named the General Sherman Tree. It stands 274 feet (83.5 meters) tall, and its trunk is 103 feet (31.4 meters) around. Scientists estimate that this tree may be 2,500 years old.

BOREAL FORESTS

Growing north of temperate coniferous and deciduous forests are boreal forests, which are also called northern coniferous forests. The word *Boreal* was the name used for the goddess of the north wind in ancient Greece. Yet another name used for boreal forests is taiga, which comes from a Russian word meaning "swampy forest."

Boreal forests, such as this forest in Alberta, Canada, grow in cold northern lands.

Where boreal forests grow

Approximately one-third of Earth's total forest area consists of boreal forest. This makes boreal forests the largest type of forest biome. Boreal forests ring the globe, occurring all around the northern hemisphere just south of the Arctic **tundra.** They are found across northern North America from northwestern Alaska to Newfoundland. Boreal forests also grow in northern Europe (including Scotland and Scandinavia) and northern Asia, in Siberia. A similar type of forest is found on high mountain slopes of all these continents, including North America's Rockies and Appalachian Mountains.

Climate

Winters in boreal forests are extremely cold and snowy. Winter temperatures typically range from −65 °F (−54 °C) to 30 °F (−1 °C). Severe cold—with average temperatures below the freezing point—may last for half the year or longer. Snowfall may cover the ground for 230 days out of the year in some areas with boreal forests.

Summers in boreal forests may sometimes be warm. Typical summer temperatures range between 20 °F and 70 °F (−7 °C and

21 °C). The organisms of a boreal forest may experience considerable temperature extremes between winter and summer. Thermometers in boreal forests in northern Minnesota have recorded temperatures of −70 °F (−57 °C) in winter and 100 °F (38 °C) in summer. The growing season in boreal forests is brief, with only 50 to 100 frost-free days during most years.

Total year-round precipitation in a boreal forest—including both rain and snow—is relatively low compared with most other forest biomes. A boreal forest typically receives roughly 15 to 30 inches (38 to 76 centimeters) of precipitation every year.

Although boreal forests do not receive a great amount of rain, the air in these forests tends to remain humid. Furthermore, many boreal forests have swamps, lakes, bogs, and other bodies of water. Such watery areas are most common in boreal forests that are in early stages of ecological succession.

The wet conditions in boreal forests are caused by two main factors. Water **evaporates** (turns from a liquid to a gas) more slowly in cool conditions than in warm conditions. Because of the generally cool weather in these forests, there is little loss of water through evaporation. In addition, the **permafrost** (permanently frozen ground beneath soil) in boreal forests prevents surface water from draining into the ground. Thus, most water remains on or just under the surface.

Boreal forests are found in parts of Asia, Europe, and North America.

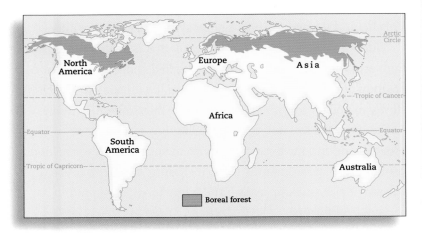

A CLOSER LOOK
The Timber Line

On mountain slopes, the highest elevation at which trees grow is called the timber line. At this level, trees occur in isolated spots, rather than in dense stands. Above the timber line, wind and cold temperatures prevent trees from growing, although mosses, shrubs, and other plants can grow there.

Bristlecone pines are trees found at timber lines in the western United States. Some bristlecone pines are known to be more than 4,600 years old.

Forests fade at the edge of the timber line on an Austrian mountain slope.

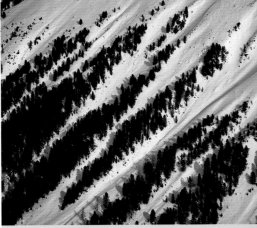

Fir trees in this boreal forest remain covered in snow for much of the year.

Plant life

Boreal forests have the simplest structure of all forest types. The plants in most other forest biomes grow in well-defined layers—called **strata**—including layers of tall trees, short trees, shrubs, and ground-level plants. A boreal forest, by contrast, basically consists of one uneven layer of trees and a layer of ground plants.

Most trees in boreal forests are evergreen conifers, such as black spruce, white spruce, jack pine, white pine, balsam fir, and hemlock. Larches (including tamarack) are deciduous conifers that are found in boreal forests. Larches shed their needlelike leaves every autumn.

The trees in many boreal forests grow so close together that a red squirrel could easily move through the forest by jumping from tree to tree without ever touching the ground. This close tree growth helps block cold winds from reaching the interior of the forest, offering protection against harsh weather for plants and animals.

Coniferous trees have a number of adaptations to help them survive in cold, snowy regions. Most conifers are shaped like a cone—narrower toward the top and wider toward the bottom. This shape helps the branches shed snow without breaking. The dark green color of conifer needles helps the needles absorb more sunlight than they would absorb if they were light in color. This helps the leaves carry out photosynthesis even in winter.

Conifers in boreal forests grow in soil that is shallow and has a high acid content. This kind of soil is called podzol soil. Decomposition of dead plant and animal material happens extremely slowly in podzol soil, and so the soil does not contain as many nutrients as the soil in temperate deciduous forests. Few broadleaf deciduous trees can survive in such soil. Nevertheless, certain broadleaf deciduous trees, including American beech, balsam poplar, quaking aspen, and white birch, are found in some boreal forests.

Boreal forests have few shrubs. Those shrubs that do grow in these forests include blueberry, cranberry, cloudberry, and crowberry—providing food for birds and other animals. The floor of boreal forests is typically covered by mosses and lichens.

Animal life

Boreal forests are most active with animal life during spring and summer. A wide variety of insects attracts many insect-eating birds, such as warblers and woodpeckers—especially during migration times. Some seed-eating birds common year-round in boreal forests are finches, sparrows, evening grosbeaks, pine siskins, and red crossbills. Water birds include loons, ducks, and geese.

Many mammals living in boreal forests belong to the weasel family, including ermine, fishers, mink, pine martens, and wolverines. Beavers often create wetland habitats in boreal forests by building dams across forest streams. Other mammals in these forests include lemmings, flying squirrels, snowshoe hare, Canada lynx, arctic foxes, wolves, and black and brown bears. Large grazing mammals include moose, caribou, reindeer, and elk (called red deer in Europe).

A red squirrel perches on a tree stump in a boreal forest. Such animals are most active during spring and summer.

TROPICAL RAIN FORESTS

Tropical rain forests are home to incredible **biodiversity.** Although these forests cover only about 6 percent of Earth's surface, scientists believe that they may contain as much as 70 percent of all species of plants and animals. Tropical rain forests, which remain warm and wet throughout the year, are found in equatorial regions (regions near the equator, the imaginary circle around Earth midway between the North and South Poles).

Large amounts of water evaporate from leaves in tropical rain forests to form clouds.

In the Western Hemisphere, tropical rain forests are found from southern Mexico to northern Brazil, in addition to several islands in the Caribbean Sea. In central Africa, tropical rain forests occur mainly in the Congo River basin, from Congo (Kinshasa) to Africa's West Coast. There are also tropical rain forests on the African island of Madagascar. In Southeast Asia, tropical rain forests grow from India to Vietnam, and in Malaysia, Indonesia, and the Philippines. Tropical rain forests also occur on New Guinea, the northeastern part of Australia, and small islands in the Pacific Ocean.

Climate

The weather in tropical rain forests stays more or less the same all year. The temperature may range from 64 °F to 95 °F (18 °C to 35 °C), though it usually stays closer to about 80 °F (27 °C). Thus, the plants and animals of a tropical rain forest do not need to adjust to great swings in temperature between the seasons, as do organisms in temperate or boreal forests.

Most tropical rain forests receive more than 80 inches (203 centimeters) of rain every year. In some areas of tropical rain forests, more than 400 inches (1,016 centimeters) of rain may fall during the year. That is more than six times the maximum amount of annual rainfall typically occurring in a temperate deciduous forest. Thunderstorms may happen more than 200 days of the year.

The relative humidity in a tropical rain forest often approaches 90 percent. Some tropical rain forests experience a brief season in which there is less rain than normal.

Rain forests and Earth

Tropical rain forests play an important role in regulating Earth's climate. Scientists have estimated that the leaves of each large tree in a tropical rain forest give off 200 gallons (757 liters) of water every year through **transpiration.** In transpiration, water evaporates from the trees' leaf pores, much like sweat evaporating on your skin. This water contributes to the formation of rain clouds.

The trees in these forests also absorb large amounts of carbon dioxide gas. Carbon dioxide is released when **fossil fuels** (coal, oil, natural gas) are burned for fuel by vehicles, factories, and power plants. Carbon dioxide traps the sun's heat near Earth's surface. This process, called the **greenhouse effect,** has caused the surface of Earth to become warmer. Scientists believe that the build-up of carbon dioxide and other **greenhouse gases** in the atmosphere is the main cause of **global warming,** the increase of Earth's average temperature. Thus, by absorbing large amounts of carbon dioxide, tropical rain forests limit global warming.

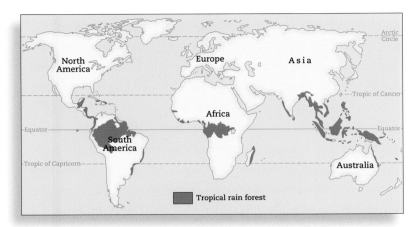

Tropical rain forests grow in regions near the equator.

Only a little light penetrates the thick canopy of a tropical rain forest and reaches the forest floor.

Structure of tropical rain forests

Unlike boreal forests, tropical rain forests have complex structures. Scientists divide the plants in tropical rain forests into five strata (layers), from top to bottom: **emergents, canopy, subcanopy, understory,** and floor.

Emergents are extremely tall trees—some more than 165 feet (50 meters) high—that are widely spaced. They receive the most sunlight, the highest temperatures, and the strongest winds in the forest. Beneath these giants are the trees of the canopy. These trees grow close together, with the crowns of the trees forming an almost continuous roof of leaves more than 65 feet (20 meters) high. Mosses, orchids, and woody vines called lianas grow on the tree branches as epiphytes. The subcanopy is a layer of shorter trees beneath the canopy.

The understory is a shady layer that is home to saplings, small palms, shrubs, and herbs. Only about 3 percent of the sunlight shining on the emergent layer reaches the understory layer, because the thick canopy blocks the rest of the light. Even less light reaches the forest floor, which is a dark place with little plant growth. Fallen leaves, branches, seeds, and fruits are found on the rain forest floor, as are fungi.

Plant life

Most trees in tropical rain forests are broadleaf evergreen trees, which continually lose their old leaves and replace them with new leaves. Many of these trees have large leaves that allow excess rain to drip off. Many trees also have large, colorful flowers and fruits.

People value rain forest trees for various products derived from them. Examples of these products include such woods as ebony, mahogany, and rosewood; such fruits as banana, coconut, grapefruit, mango, and pineapple; and cocoa, coffee, and rubber. Popular houseplants derived from the rain forest understory include ferns, palms, and philodendrons (*FIHL uh DEHN druhns*).

The capybara is the world's largest rodent. It lives in Central and South America.

Animal life

The most plentiful animals in tropical rain forests are insects, including thousands of species of ants, beetles, and butterflies. Researchers identified more than 1,200 species of beetles living on only 19 rain forest trees in Panama. Large tarantulas are also found in tropical rain forests.

Lakes and rivers in tropical rain forests contain numerous fish, including the flesh-eating piranha (*pih RAHN yuh*) and the arapaima (*ar uh PY muh*), one of the largest freshwater fish in the world. Amphibians include small, colorful tree frogs, such as arrow-poison frogs. Among the many rain forest reptiles are iguanas and giant snakes, such as anacondas—which may grow as long as 30 feet (9 meters).

Thousands of species of brightly colored birds fly through tropical rain forest canopies, including macaws, parrots, peacocks, and toucans. Bats and monkeys also live in the canopies. In South American rain forests, there are ocelots (*OH suh lots*), sloths, tapirs (*TAY peers*), and the capybara, the world's largest rodent. In Africa, chimpanzees, gorillas, lemurs, and elephants live in rain forests. Asian rain forests are home to orangutans, gibbons, tigers, and elephants.

The world's largest flower grows in rain forests in Asia. This flower, called rafflesia (*ra FLEE zhuh*), can grow to be more than 3 feet (90 centimeters) wide. The plant has no leaves or stems; instead, its large flowers grow on the stems and roots of shrubs.

The rafflesia flower gives off an odor similar to rotting flesh, attracting such meat-eating insects as carrion flies and beetles. These insects spread pollen from male to female rafflesia flowers.

Trees in tropical seasonal forests, such as these bao-babs in Madagascar, lose their leaves during the dry season.

TROPICAL SEASONAL FORESTS

Tropical seasonal forests are found farther away from the equator than tropical rain forests—typically in areas between tropical rain forests and savannas (biomes consisting of grassland and a few widely separated trees). Tropical seasonal forests have fewer trees than tropical rain forests, but more trees than savannas.

Tropical seasonal forests grow in Mexico, on the west coast of Central America, and in central South America. These forests are also in parts of central and southern Africa, India, Sri Lanka, Vietnam, China, and northern Australia, as well as on some small islands in the Pacific Ocean. Regions with tropical seasonal forests have some of the fastest-growing human populations. These forests are increasingly threatened by people who clear them to make room for homes, farms, and ranches.

Changing seasons

Tropical seasonal forests, like temperate deciduous forests, have weather that changes dramatically with the seasons. But instead of changing between hot and cold seasons, tropical seasonal forests change between wet and dry seasons.

The wetter season, which occurs in summer, is called the wet

monsoon season. During this period, monsoon winds carry moisture from seawater evaporation over the land. The moisture rises high into the atmosphere, where it forms rain clouds. These clouds cause intense rainfall in summer.

In winter, the monsoon winds change direction, so the dry air over the land blows offshore to the sea. The resulting drier season is called the dry monsoon season. Very little rain may fall during this time. Because of the monsoon winds that influence their weather, tropical seasonal forests are also called monsoon forests.

Climate

Depending on the region in which it lies, a tropical seasonal forest may receive between about 20 inches and 118 inches (50 centimeters and 300 centimeters) of rain per year. Some tropical seasonal forests receive as much rain as certain tropical rain forests, but the rain in a tropical rain forest is spread evenly throughout the year. In Costa Rica's Santa Rosa National Park—a typical tropical seasonal forest—the rainiest month is usually May, the first month of the wet monsoon season. Heavy rains in this forest then continue into November, after which the dry monsoon season begins.

Average temperatures in tropical seasonal forests range between 68 °F and 86 °F (20 °C and 30 °C), depending on the forest's location. The temperatures in any particular tropical seasonal forest vary only slightly. The highest temperatures tend to occur right before the beginning of rainy periods. Once the rain starts, cloud cover causes temperatures to fall.

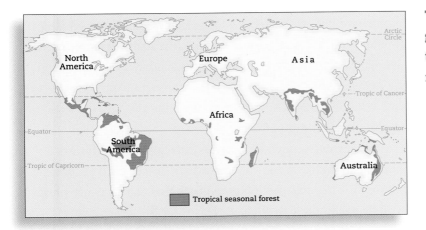

Tropical seasonal forest

Tropical seasonal forests generally grow farther from the equator than tropical rain forests.

Acacia trees, such as these in Kenya's Nakuru National Park, are specially adapted to wet and dry extremes.

Life in tropical seasonal forests

The plants and animals of a tropical seasonal forest are adapted to survive the precipitation extremes of this biome—months of heavy rains followed by months of drought. Most of the trees in these forests are broadleaf deciduous trees. However, these trees are unlike broadleaf trees in a temperate deciduous forest, which shed their leaves to help them preserve energy during the cold season. The broadleaf trees in a tropical seasonal forest shed their leaves to help them make it through the dry season. Leaves lose water through transpiration. Thus, without their leaves, the trees can save whatever scarce water is available. Animals in tropical seasonal forests are also specially adapted to the wet and dry extremes.

Plant life

The canopy of a tropical seasonal forest is roughly 100 feet (30 meters) high. It is much more open than the canopy of a tropical rain forest, allowing abundant sunlight to reach the forest floor. As a result, there is a great deal of undergrowth in a tropical seasonal forest, including many shrubs, herbs, and grasses.

Acacias (*uh KAY shuhs*) are among the most fascinating trees and shrubs found in tropical seasonal forests. Some of these plants have hollow thorns in which ants live. The ants, which eat sweet nectar secreted by glands in the leaf stalks, are very aggressive. They sting insects and other animals that try to browse on the tree, and they bite away vines that try to grow on the tree. This kind of relationship, in which both the tree and the ants benefit, is called **mutualism.**

Another interesting tree in some tropical seasonal forests is indio desnudo (meaning "naked Indian"), also called gumbo-limbo. This tree has peeling green bark that can carry out photosynthesis after the tree sheds its leaves for the dry season.

Animal life

Like the trees, some of the animals in a tropical seasonal forest spend the dry season in an inactive state, called **estivation**, that protects them from dryness. Estivation is similar to the way certain northern animals hibernate to protect themselves from cold. When an animal estivates, its breathing, heartbeat, and other body functions slow down as it "sleeps" in a hiding place. When the rains return, the animal becomes active again.

Reptiles that live in tropical seasonal forests include several colorful lizards, such as anoles, iguanas, and ctenosaurs. Beautiful birds that live in tropical seasonal forests include the blue-crowned motmot, crested guan, magpie-jay, and squirrel cuckoo. In South American tropical seasonal forests, mammals include the agouti (a large rodent), the coati (a relative of the raccoon), and howler and capuchin monkeys. In Africa, such well-known mammals as giraffes and rhinoceroses roam tropical seasonal forests. Kangaroos hop through these forests in Australia.

A ring-tailed lemur perches on a branch in a tropical seasonal forest.

A CLOSER LOOK
Monsoons and Agriculture

People in southern Asia rely on monsoons for agriculture. These winds, which blow from the northern part of the Indian Ocean, bring heavy rains that fertilize the soil, which makes it possible to grow crops. However, abnormally strong monsoons can destroy much of the crops and livestock in such countries as Bangladesh, India, Myanmar, and Thailand.

Each year, meteorologists try to predict the timing of monsoon rains so that farmers can plant crops at the best time. Too little or too much rain can destroy the crops and lead to dwindling food supplies for the region's inhabitants.

Farmers in India stand over a crop field damaged by monsoon floods.

LOGGING

Forests once covered approximately 60 percent of Earth's surface. Today, they cover only about 30 percent. During the past several thousand years, vast areas of forest have been cleared for farms and cities. This loss has greatly increased since the 1800's. According to the U.S. Department of State, an area of forest four times the size of Switzerland is lost every year because of **deforestation** (the clearing of trees) or **degradation** (damage caused by such factors as pollution, mining, and oil drilling).

A type of logging called clearcutting removes all the trees from an area, destroying its natural ecosystem.

Types of logging

Most deforestation occurs in regions experiencing rapid population growth, such as South America, central Africa, and Southeast Asia. Millions of acres of tropical forests in these regions are destroyed each year to make room for farms, cattle ranches, towns, and dams, and to harvest the timber.

Timber harvesting—or logging—is a major cause of deforestation throughout the world. Trees are cut down to manufacture lumber, paper, cardboard, and other products. One study found that a large fast food company needs to harvest 800 square miles (2,072 square kilometers) of trees to make enough paper for a year's supply of packaging.

The most damaging form of logging is **clearcutting**, in which all the trees in an area are removed. This practice completely destroys the natural ecosystem of the area. Even when all the trees in an area are not removed, the forest may become fragmented—meaning that the remaining stands of trees are like widely separated islands. When this happens, wild animals have difficulty moving through the area in search of food.

Effects of logging

The destruction of forests has placed many species of plants and animals in danger of extinction. The black rhinoceros is one such example, with only about 3,000 black rhinos remaining in the wild. Only about 720 mountain gorillas remain in their forest habitats. Fewer than 2,500 lion-tailed macaques survive. The Amur tiger (also called the Siberian tiger) is particularly threatened, with only about 250 individuals of this species remaining.

Another result of deforestation is the loss of an area's topsoil and its network of plant roots. Topsoil and roots absorb and trap runoff from rainwater and melting snow—thus preventing flooding. With the destruction of a region's forests, flooding increases in the area.

Conservation

Governments around the world have established nature reserves to protect some forests. In the United States, the U.S. Forest Service manages numerous national forests. Any logging in these forests must be performed in a **sustainable** manner—that is, enough trees of various species and ages must be saved to protect the ecosystem.

Besides government actions, there have also been changes in industrial logging policies to take ecological factors into account. For example, loggers often leave strips of forest standing that connect fragmented areas of deforested land. These strips form pathways for the movement of forest-dwelling animals.

A number of international **conservation** organizations work with governments and local groups to protect forests. Among these conservation organizations are the Nature Conservancy and the World Wildlife Fund.

Travelers hike through a protected area of forest in Malaysia's Bako National Park.

Slash-and-burn agriculture ruins forests and depletes nutrients in the soil.

FARMING

Deforestation is often performed in regions with tropical rain forests to make land that is suitable for growing crops or raising livestock. Millions of people in these regions depend on farming or ranching for their livelihoods. Some of these people are **subsistence farmers**, farming the land just to grow enough food for themselves. Others work as field laborers for large international corporations.

Slash-and-burn

In a destructive procedure called **slash-and-burn agriculture**, farmers first cut down all the trees in an area of rain forest. They then burn the dead trees to break them down into chemical nutrients, which serve as **fertilizers** for the soil. These nutrients allow the farmers to grow crops on the land for a short period—perhaps a year or two. However, the nutrients quickly become depleted, leaving the soil barren (unable to grow crops). After the soil in one area becomes barren, the farmers move to a new area. There, they repeat their slash-and-burn techniques.

Monocultures and ranching

Another destructive agricultural practice is the planting of **monocultures** on land that was formerly rain forest. Monocultures consist of large farm areas in which only a single kind of crop is planted. The replacement of the rich biodiversity of a rain forest by a farm field growing a single crop is ecologically devastating for a region.

Monocultures are also harmful for the rest of the world. A field planted with a monoculture does not remove as much carbon dioxide from the atmosphere as a mature rain forest. Thus, monocultures contribute to global warming.

One of the main monoculture crops grown on rain forest land, especially in Brazil, is sugar cane. Sugar cane is often used to make **ethanol**, a type of alcohol that is used as a fuel for automobiles. Another crop grown as a monoculture is soybean. Soybeans are used to produce food for both human and livestock consumption. Yet another monoculture crop is the oil palm, which is used in foods ranging from potato chips to chocolate bars.

When rain forest land is cleared for cattle ranching, the land is replanted with pasture grasses for grazing. Most of the cattle raised on such land are used to produce beef that is exported to the United States and other countries.

Conservation

Governments of many nations are working to protect forests from harmful agricultural practices. In 2006, the government of Brazil placed 58,000 square miles (150,000 square kilometers) of rain forest under protection. Conservation International, a conservation organization based in Washington, D.C., helped fund this preservation action. In order for such actions to be effective, however, subsistence farmers need to be offered other ways to make a living besides clearing forests.

Monocultures, such as this soybean field in the Amazon rain forest, separate areas of healthy forest and reduce biodiversity.

Acid rain, which forms from pollutants in the air, can devastate forests.

INDUSTRIAL POLLUTION

Industrial pollution consists of harmful substances released into the environment by such activities as manufacturing, electricity generation, the use of agricultural and household chemicals, and the driving of automobiles. Among the many forms of industrial pollution are **acid rain**, **smog**, dangerous chemicals in waterways, and spills of toxic substances. All of these forms of pollution harm forests.

Acid rain and smog

Acid rain is rain or snow that is acidic in nature. The degree of acidity in a substance is given by a number on the **pH scale**, which ranges from 0 to 14. A substance with a pH factor of 7 is neutral—neither acidic nor alkaline (basic). A solution with a pH factor below 7, such as orange juice and vinegar, is acidic, while a solution with a pH factor above 7, such as ammonia and baking soda, is alkaline.

Rainwater normally has a neutral pH factor. However, certain chemical **pollutants** cause rain to have an acidic pH factor. Sulfur dioxide and nitrogen oxides are released into the air by the burning of fossil fuels. These substances mix with water vapor in the air, forming sulfuric acid and nitric acid. When precipitation containing these acids falls on plants, photosynthesis may be disrupted. The plants then become weak and less resistant to disease.

Smog consists mostly of a gas called **ozone.** It forms when nitrogen oxides and other substances released by the burning of fossil fuels undergo chemical changes in sunlight. When smog enters the stomata (pores) of leaves, it damages plant proteins, reduces seed production, and makes the plants more sensitive to drought and disease.

Runoff and spills

Various kinds of harmful chemicals, such as **pesticides** used on farms and in yards, collect in runoff water that flows into forests. In forest streams and lakes, such chemicals can cause disease and death in wildlife. In forest soil, the chemicals may be taken up by the roots of plants, killing the plants or stunting their growth.

Oil and other toxic substances are sometimes spilled onto forest land. When such substances get into the soil, an area can become so contaminated that plants will be unable to grow there for many years.

Fighting pollution

Power plants and factories that burn fossil fuels can reduce the amount of pollutants released into the atmosphere by using devices called **scrubbers.** These devices act like filters to remove harmful substances from boiler gases before the gases leave smokestacks. Catalytic converters are devices on automobiles that reduce pollutants in exhaust fumes.

In the United States, the Clean Air Act requires that industries reduce pollution to combat acid rain. In addition, the United States is part of an international agreement, called the Long-Range Transboundary Air Pollution Agreement, designed to reduce acid rain and smog. The Clean Water Act helps protect water supplies in U.S. forests.

A Nigerian child holds oil that has spilled into a forested region near a river delta.

Type of pollution	Sources
Acid rain	Sulfur dioxide and nitrogen oxides from burning of fossil fuels* mix with water vapor in the air
Smog	Nitrogen oxides and other substances from burning of fossil fuels* undergo chemical changes in sunlight
Carbon dioxide, other greenhouse gases	Emissions from the burning of fossil fuels*
Pesticides, fertilizers	Agriculture and residential chemical use
Chlorofluorocarbons	Old refrigerants, plastic foam insulation
Petroleum	Oil spills
Toxic metal compounds	Various industrial processes, solid waste incineration
Hazardous wastes	Various industrial processes, hospital and laboratory wastes
Human sewage/ animal wastes	Untreated runoff from cities and farms

* Fossil fuels are burned by factories, power plants, and automobiles.

WARFARE

War can be extremely destructive to forest ecosystems. Throughout history, human beings have used forests and forest products in warfare. People used wood to make such weapons as bows and arrows, clubs, and spears. People also used wood as fuel in furnaces for forging metal weapons. Cyprus, an area near the Mediterranean Sea, lost most of its forests by 1200 B.C. because so many people used wood for making copper.

People have also long used timber to create defensive fortifications. In ancient Japan, castles were traditionally made of wood. By the 1600's, people in Japan had used so much timber that wood shortages became a problem across the country.

Armies throughout history have burned forests to clear enemies living or fighting there. But modern technology has allowed human beings to cause vastly more forest destruction than ever before. The use of **chemical warfare** agents and the enormous firepower of modern weaponry can leave forests barren.

Before (top) and after (bottom) photos show the devastation caused by Agent Orange to this mangrove forest in Vietnam.

Fighting guerrillas

Guerrillas are fighters who typically hide out in forests and other natural areas. Guerrillas often use such natural cover to mount sneak attacks against a stronger, better-equipped army. When fighting guerrillas, armies and government forces focus their firepower on the natural areas where they hide.

During the Vietnam War (1957-1975), the United States military sprayed 21 million gallons (79 million liters) of an **herbicide** (plant-killing substance) called Agent Orange over the tropical seasonal forests of southern Vietnam. By killing the trees and dense foliage, the U.S. military hoped to deprive Communist guerrillas of their hiding places. Some of these sprayed forests have since recovered, but others remain only scrubby grassland. Agent Orange also caused cancer and other diseases among

Rwandan refugees use wood for fuel. War can indirectly cause huge damage to forests.

people exposed to the substance.

Refugees and poaching

The mass migration of **refugees** fleeing fighting also causes ecological damage. In the 1990's, more than 2 million refugees fled fighting in the African nation of Rwanda. Many of the refugees set up camps in the tropical rain forests of central Africa. Within one six-month period, refugees and soldiers stripped 116 square miles (300 square kilometers) of rain forest for firewood, shelter, and food.

Bands of fighters in other conflicts in Africa have poached (illegally killed) elephants to obtain ivory tusks for sale. In still other conflicts, fighters have polluted forests by blowing up oil pipelines and mines.

Conservation efforts

In 1992, the **United Nations' (UN)** Rio Declaration condemned environmental destruction caused by warfare. Conservation organizations sometimes work with governments to protect natural areas from war. Concerns about environmental problems, however, are often ignored when government officials are more worried about national security.

A CLOSER LOOK

The Rio Declaration

The Rio Declaration on Environment and Development was produced in 1992 at a United Nations conference. It contains 27 principles guiding international cooperation on economic development and environmental protection. Principle 24 states: "Warfare is inherently destructive of sustainable development. States shall therefore respect international law providing protection for the environment in times of armed conflict and cooperate in its further development, as necessary."

United Nations leaders gathered at the Earth Summit in Rio de Janeiro, Brazil.

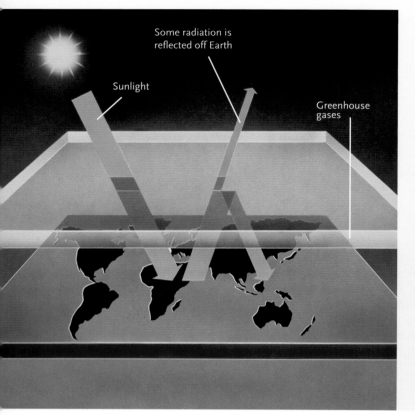

Sunlight

Some radiation is reflected off Earth

Greenhouse gases

CLIMATE CHANGE

Many scientists believe that Earth is entering a period of global warming. Earth's climate has changed many times in the past, back and forth from ice ages to periods of tropical warmth. But today, scientists warn that the planet is warming so quickly that living things may not be able to adapt.

Global warming is caused by **greenhouse gases,** such as carbon dioxide, that build up in Earth's atmosphere and trap the sun's heat. Oil-based fuels for vehicles, coal in power plants, and many other modern sources of energy release carbon dioxide as they are burned. Forests help prevent global warming by absorbing carbon dioxide.

Greenhouse gases, such as carbon dioxide, build up in the atmosphere and trap the sun's heat.

Some natural sources, such as volcanoes, also produce carbon dioxide. But most scientists agree that human activities are the main cause of a build-up of greenhouse gases in the atmosphere today. In 2007, the Intergovernmental Panel on Climate Change (IPCC), a group of climate experts sponsored by the United Nations, concluded that human beings have almost certainly caused most of the global warming since the 1950's.

Global warming's effects on forests

At least one-third of Earth's remaining forests may be affected by global warming, according to the IPCC. Scientists have already observed a number of changes in forests that may be related to changes in climate. Some bird species have altered the timing and geographical ranges of their migrations. The flowering and fruiting times of certain plants have also changed.

Disease-causing germs and disease-carrying insects become more common in warmer weather. Scientists have reported that the number of trees weakened or killed by bark beetles has soared in the boreal forests of British Columbia and Alaska. Bark beetles lay eggs—and spread fungal diseases—beneath tree bark. According to researchers, milder weather has allowed more bark beetles to survive the northern winters.

Shifting forests

As weather becomes warmer, forests in certain regions may give way to other biome types better suited to the changed conditions. For example, boreal forests may be replaced by temperate deciduous forests as their northern range becomes warmer. In turn, temperate deciduous forests may be replaced by grasslands as their range warms and becomes drier.

Some forests may expand in area as the climate warms. Experiments have shown that some trees benefit from high concentrations of carbon dioxide in the atmosphere by increasing their leaf, seed, and fruit production.

Fighting global warming

Countries around the world are trying to slow the effects of global warming by reducing **emissions** of carbon dioxide and other greenhouse gases by power plants, automobiles, and other sources. The **Kyoto Protocol** is an international agreement requiring industrialized nations to reduce greenhouse gas emissions to certain levels.

The Intergovernmental Panel on Climate Change (IPCC) is an international scientific group established by the United Nations to assess findings about climate change. The IPCC produces reports that are used by government officials to make policies regarding global warming, such as **regulations** on greenhouse gas emissions.

Trees in boreal forests are increasingly harmed by bark beetles, which spread farther north as the climate warms.

What Are Wetlands?

Section Summary

A wetland is an area of land in which the ground remains soaked with water or submerged beneath it for most of the year.

Many wetlands have been destroyed or polluted in the process of land development. Introduced plants or animals also endanger wetlands.

Global warming could cause significant damage to wetlands, from increased flooding and droughts to a deterioration of water quality.

A wetland in central Nicaragua forms along a winding river.

Wetlands are often beautiful, busy, and distinctive environments. Sunlight glistens off the water surface between stands of tall cattails and bulrushes. The air is filled with the sounds of croaking frogs, quacking ducks, buzzing dragonflies, and the trill-sounding *konk-la-reeee* calls of red-winged blackbirds. Muskrats sit atop their lodges—piles of twigs and grasses in the middle of the water.

Where wetlands are found

A wetland is any area of land in which the ground remains soaked with **ground water** or submerged under surface water for much or all of the year. The water in a wetland is typically shallower than that in a lake or pond. In addition, unlike a typical lake or pond, a wetland may be dry for part of the year.

Wetlands are found around the world in both cold and warm climates, from the Arctic **tundra** to the tropics. The only continent with no wetlands is Antarctica. Many wetlands are in low inland floodplains (flat land that sometimes floods) near lakes and rivers. Such wetlands contain fresh water. Other wetlands are near seacoasts. These wetlands usually contain a mixture of fresh water and salt water, called brackish water.

Types of wetlands

There are several different types of wetlands, including marshes, swamps, bogs, and fens. The types found in any region depend on several factors, such as climate, soil, and the shape of the landscape. Each wetland type has characteristic kinds of plants and animals.

Marshes look like flooded grasslands, with many species of grasses and grasslike plants. There are usually few or no trees in marshes. Marshes are found both inland and along seacoasts. Swamps are areas of forest that are flooded for much of the year. Trees and shrubs are the main plants in swamps. Like marshes, swamps may occur both inland and by seacoasts.

Bogs and fens are areas covered by wet, spongy mats of peat (partially decayed plant material). They are usually found in regions with colder climates. Bog water and soil are usually very acidic, with few nutrients. Fen water and soil, on the other hand, are usually less acidic, containing more nutrients. Some plants in these **habitats** have special ways to obtain nutrients—such as by capturing and digesting insects.

Wetlands are home to a great variety of animals. Some animals—such as crayfish, snails, fish, frogs, turtles, alligators, waterfowl, and many insects—spend their entire lives in wetlands. Other animals use wetlands only for special purposes, such as foraging, hunting, drinking, or breeding. Such animals include minks, raccoons, foxes, and deer. Wetlands are very important to many species of migrating birds, which use these habitats for resting and feeding during their long journeys every spring and fall.

Wetlands in Georgia's Cumberland Island National Seashore contain both salt water and fresh water.

WETLAND ECOLOGY

Although each kind of wetland has its own unique traits, some general features apply to most wetland **ecosystems.** Wetland plants are classified into categories based on where they grow. Some plants, called **emergents**, grow above the water surface. These may include cattails, sedges, arrowheads, and pickerelweeds. The leaves of floating plants, such as duckweeds and water lilies, lie flat on the water surface. **Submergents** are plants, such as water milfoil and coontail (also called hornwort), that remain mostly or completely underwater. Many species of algae are also found floating and submerged in wetlands.

Wetlands contain many unique plants and animals, such as water lilies (above) and the Acadian hairstreak butterfly (below).

Wetland food chains

As in a forest, energy in wetlands flows through interconnected **food chains** consisting of **producers, consumers,** and **decomposers.** Primary producers in a wetland include both algae and plants, which create their own food through **photosynthesis.** Primary consumers may include insect **larvae**, which eat the algae and plants. Secondary consumers typically include small fish, such as sunfish and shiners, which eat the insect larvae. Tertiary consumers consist of predatory animals, such as largemouth bass and raccoons, which eat the small fish.

Bacteria, fungi, and worms in wetlands carry out **decomposition** of dead plant and animal material in the waterlogged soil. However, such soil contains less oxygen than the drier soil in forests and other land **biomes.** Bacteria require oxygen to decompose efficiently. Thus, decomposition occurs at a slower rate in wetlands than in other areas. This is especially true in the acidic soil of bogs, where well-preserved animal and human remains hundreds of years old have been discovered.

Importance of wetlands

Wetland ecosystems are beneficial to people. Wetlands act like sponges that absorb rainwater and snowmelt flowing across the land's surface. This absorption reduces the extent and heights of floods in an area. Wetland plants act like brakes to slow the surging flow of surface water from storms. This braking action reduces the loss of a region's topsoil through erosion (wearing away by wind or water). Along seacoasts, wetlands protect shorelines from erosion.

Wetlands are often compared with the kidneys of the human body. Kidneys filter harmful wastes out of the blood. Wetlands filter harmful **pollutants** and sediments out of runoff water flowing from higher ground. These substances are absorbed by wetlands before they can reach ground water or open water supplies used by people.

Healthy wetland ecosystems are sources of many natural products used by people. Fish and shellfish come from some wetlands, as do blueberries and cranberries. Medicines are derived from some wetland plants, and furs and skins are obtained from some wetland animals.

Wetland plants and animals have evolved to thrive in damp conditions.

The water level in tidal marshes, such as this area in Florida, rises and falls with the tides.

MARSHES

Marshes are wetlands dominated by soft-stemmed, non-woody plants, such as grasses and cattails. A marsh with a great deal of vegetation looks like a wet grassland. In a typical marsh, there are no shrubs or trees.

Types of marshes

Marshes that occur inland, called nontidal marshes, consist of fresh water. Marshes along seacoasts, called tidal marshes or salt marshes, consist of a mixture of fresh water and salt water.

Freshwater marshes are more common and widespread than salt marshes. They are found throughout the world in nonwooded places where shallow water—usually a few inches to a few feet—remains above ground for most or all of the year. Freshwater marshes are usually located along the shores of lakes, ponds, rivers, or streams. Most of the water in a freshwater marsh comes from the surface, such as floodwater from lakes and rivers and runoff from rain and melted snow.

Special types of freshwater marshes exist in some places. Prairie potholes are depressions that dot the landscape like pockmarks in the upper Midwest of the United States. They usually fill in with rainwater and snowmelt in spring. Playa lakes are a similar type of temporary marsh in the southern Great Plains region. Vernal pools are small, seasonal marshes that are common in California.

Marsh life

Because the surface runoff that feeds freshwater marshes carries many nourishing chemicals, the soil in these ecosystems is rich in nutrients. The rich soil supports a great diversity of emergent plants, including grasses, reeds, sedges, cattails, bulrushes, and horsetails. Water lilies, including lotus plants, are common floating plants, while various kinds of pondweeds are present as both floaters and submergents.

Dragonflies, damselflies, mayflies, and other insects lay their eggs in freshwater marshes, where the young insects, called naiads (*NAY yuh DEEs*), or water larvae, develop underwater. Northern pike and other fish use freshwater marshes as egg-laying and nursery habitats. Frog tadpoles and other young amphibians also develop in marsh waters.

Numerous songbirds, such as the red-winged blackbird and common yellowthroat, are often seen perched on plants in freshwater marshes. Common wading birds in marshes include herons, egrets, cranes, and rails, while **raptors** include the osprey and marsh hawk. Marsh mammals in North America include muskrats, beavers, otters, and mink. In South America, the capybara (*KAP uh BAHR uh*) and coypu are large rodents that live in freshwater marshes.

Salt marshes occur where fresh water flows into the sea, such as at a river mouth. The water level in salt marshes rises and falls twice a day with changes in the tides. Plants growing in these marshes, including cordgrass, salt-meadow grass, and spike grass, are adapted to high salt concentrations. Many fish and shellfish breed in salt marshes, including flounder, menhaden (*mehn HAY duhn*), sea trout, striped bass, shrimp, oysters, clams, and crabs.

Marshes are wetlands dominated by nonwoody plants, such as grasses and cattails.

SWAMPS

Swamps are wetlands with trees and shrubs. They are found in inland and coastal areas that have shallow standing or slowly flowing water for at least part of the year. There are various kinds of swamps—some containing fresh water, others containing a mixture of fresh water and salt water.

A freshwater swamp develops gradually, often starting out as a lake or pond surrounded by a forest. Over time, trees and shrubs take root closer and closer to the water—then in the shallow bottom of the lake or pond. As the plants die, their remains sink to the bottom, causing the bed of the lake or pond to build up closer to the surface. More trees can then take root, forming a swamp. A swamp may also form when a curve in a forest stream gets cut off from the main channel. The resulting "oxbow lake" eventually fills in with sediment and plants.

Standing water soaks the soil of this Texas swamp. Baldcypress trees form "knees" that stay above the water.

Swamp plants

Bottomland hardwood swamps are common freshwater swamps in forest floodplains in the southeastern and south-central United States. Some of the trees that grow in these occasionally flooded areas are overcup oak, water tupelo and other gum trees, and baldcypress, a deciduous conifer.

Cypress swamps, located mostly along river and lake margins in the eastern and southern United States, are dominated by baldcypress. These trees are usually draped with vines, orchids, Spanish moss, and other **epiphytes.**

Baldcypress trees have woody "knees," called pneumatophores (*new MAT a FORs*) that stick out of the stagnant, low-oxygen water. These knees are parts of the trees' roots. Mangrove trees, which grow in salt marshes along coasts, also have extensive pneumatophores. The pneumatophores help support the trees in unstable wetland soils, and in mangroves they also absorb oxygen from the air.

Red maple swamps are common in the northeastern United States. Besides red maple, the main trees that grow in these swamps include pin oak and gum trees. In shrub swamps, such shrubs as buttonbush, dogwood, and willow are more common than trees.

Swamp animals

The wildlife of freshwater swamps includes many insects, crayfish, snails, and clams. Alligators, crocodiles, and snapping turtles are examples of swamp reptiles. Poisonous snakes, such as the copperhead and water moccasin (also called cottonmouth), are found in southern U.S. swamps. Swamp birds include herons, kingfishers, wood ducks, hawks, and owls. Several endangered species of mammals live in swampy regions in the southeastern United States, including the Florida panther and red wolf.

Mangrove swamps are found along seacoasts in tropical and subtropical regions. The trees' stilt-like roots form spreading clusters along the coasts, which provide shelter for many young fish and such marine **invertebrates** as oysters and barnacles.

A tricolored heron stands in swamp water. Such wading birds depend on water-dwelling animals for food.

BOGS AND FENS

Bogs and fens are wetlands that grow in many cool, wet, northern regions. Bacteria have trouble breaking down organic (plant and animal) remains in such conditions. Without such decomposition, partially decayed organic material builds up in bogs and fens. This material forms a spongy substance called **peat**. The peat may form mats that float on the surface of water.

All or most of the water in bogs comes from **precipitation.** On the other hand, the water in fens comes from water draining into the area from higher ground, often through ground water. The water in bogs is acidic. But a fen's water contains dissolved minerals that make it less acidic than that of a bog.

Thick mats of moss and peat float on the standing water in this Massachusetts bog.

Bogs

Only specialized plants can grow in the acidic, low-oxygen, low-nutrient soil of bogs. Some of these plants are **carnivores**, capturing and digesting insects and other small animals. For example, insects landing on the wet leaves of a pitcher plant slide into a pool of water within the "pitcher" formed by the plant's leaves. Bacteria in this pool break down the insects into nitrogen and other nutritious chemical substances, which the plant then absorbs. Other carnivorous plants in bogs are bladderworts, butterworts, and sundews.

A bog's peaty surface is usually covered with a layer of sphagnum (*SFAG nuhm*) moss. Other plants, such as cotton grass, cranberry, blueberry, leatherleaf, and Labrador tea, are specially adapted to the acidic conditions in bogs. Most trees growing in bogs are conifers, including tamarack, black spruce, and pines. Some of the evergreen trees and shrubs in bogs grow in stunted form.

Bogs are home to numerous species of insects, including many beetles, butterflies, dragonflies, and mosquitoes. These insects serve as food for the many insect-eating birds common to bogs, such as flycatchers, kinglets, nuthatches, and wood warblers. Other bog birds include the sandhill crane, sora rail, osprey, and great gray owl. The massasauga (*MAS uh SAW guh*) rattlesnake and snapping and spotted turtles are some bog reptiles. Mammals found in bogs include water shrews, bog lemmings, muskrats, lynx, black bears, and moose. Few fish are found in the low-oxygen water of bogs.

Fens

Fens typically have more diverse plant species than bogs. In fens, there may be a ground cover of various grasses, sedges and rushes (grasslike plants), shrubs, and such wildflowers as showy ladyslipper and spreading globeflower, as well as white cedar trees. The richest growth of such plants occurs in areas of fens that are the least acidic. Areas of fens that are more acidic have plants similar to those found in bogs. In some fens, plants grow in a pattern of parallel ridges of abundant vegetation separated by areas with less vegetation. The abundant growth occurs in those places that have the most nutrients left by the flow of water through the soil.

Animal species in fens are similar to species found in bogs. However, the surface water outflows of fens are sometimes home to newly hatched fish, such as brook trout. These outflows also attract beavers, with their instinct for building dams.

Fens are similar to bogs, but their water contains dissolved minerals that make them less acidic.

A reservoir being built in Florida's Everglades aims to restore a more natural water flow to the area.

HUMAN SETTLEMENT

Since 1800, people have drained and destroyed more than half the wetlands that existed in the continental United States. These wetlands were destroyed to make room for farms, cities, and roads. They were also destroyed as a way to fight malaria and other diseases carried by mosquitoes, which breed in wetlands. Wetlands have been drained and filled in throughout the world for similar reasons. Fortunately, people have increasingly become aware of the ecological importance of wetlands and are now working to save wetland habitats.

The Everglades

The Everglades provide an example of how human settlement has harmed wetlands. The Everglades, in southern Florida, are among the most unique wetland regions in the world. They formed when the water from melting glaciers raised sea levels after the end of the last ice age, about 11,500 years ago. Today the Everglades consist of various kinds of wetland ecosystems, including freshwater marshes, salt marshes, and mangrove swamps.

Much of the Everglades was drained during the 1900's to make land for growing vegetables and sugar cane. In addition, many canals were built in the Everglades to supply water to the growing human population in the Miami region. In the 1960's, engineers altered the natural flow of the Kissimmee River, the major source of water for the southern Everglades, by forcing its waters into a straight, concrete canal.

All of these actions had disastrous effects on the Everglades. Many areas dried up completely, and a number of plant and animal species became threatened with extinction. Among the many endangered species in the Everglades are the American crocodile, the wood stork, the Florida panther, and the West Indian manatee. **Pesticides** and other chemical substances carried in runoff water from farms and homes have polluted the Everglades. Also, many species of nonnative plants, which people introduced into the area from elsewhere, have crowded out native species in the Everglades.

Preservation efforts

In 1999, the U.S. Army Corps of Engineers began work on a 20-year project to restore the Everglades to a more natural condition. This work involves such actions as removing drainage canals and other artificial structures to allow the Everglades' waters to flow more naturally. Officials with the Florida state government are also working on Everglades restoration projects.

The Everglades restoration efforts are among many actions being taken to preserve or restore wetlands in the United States and other countries. In the United States, a number of laws protect wetlands by regulating private practices in and around wetlands. More than 150 nations are parties to the 1971 Ramsar Convention on Wetlands, an international agreement that encourages the **conservation** and wise use of wetlands. This agreement names hundreds of wetlands around the world as being especially important for ecological reasons.

The Florida Everglades

A map of the Florida Everglades showing cities including Bradenton, Sarasota, Port Charlotte, Fort Myers, Naples, Sebring, Fort Pierce, Port St. Lucie, Okeechobee, Moore Haven, West Palm Beach, Fort Lauderdale, and Miami. Features labeled include the Gulf of Mexico, Atlantic Ocean, Lake Okeechobee, Lake Istokpoga, Lake Placid, Lake Trafford, Charlotte Harbor, Myakka River, Peace River, Kissimmee River, Caloosahatchee R., St. Lucie Canal, Hillsboro Canal, Miami Canal, North New River Canal, Tamiami Canal, Planned restoration area for Everglades "river of grass", Florida Panther Natl. Wildlife Refuge, Arthur R. Marshall Loxahatchee National Wildlife Refuge, Big Cypress National Preserve, Water Conservation Area 3, W.C.A. 1, W.C.A. 2, Everglades National Park, Biscayne National Park, Biscayne Bay, Ponce de Leon Bay, Cape Sable, Florida Bay. A scale shows 0 to 40 Miles and 0 to 40 Kilometers. A legend marks Urban area and North. An inset map shows the United States with Alabama, Georgia, Florida, Atlantic Ocean, Gulf of Mexico, and the Everglades area of detail map (Everglades National Park).

The Florida panther belongs to the same species (*Puma concolor*) as big cats that are called cougars, mountain lions, pumas, painters, and catamounts in other regions. Cougars once lived throughout the United States, Southern Canada, and Mexico, but hunting and habitat destruction have dramatically reduced their populations. By the late 1800's, the remaining cougars east of the Rocky Mountains lived mainly in Texas and Florida.

In southern Florida, human settlement and pollution continue to reduce the panther's habitat and threaten its populations. Currently, only 30 to 50 Florida panthers live in the wild.

Untreated phosphorus pollutes the Po River in Italy. The chemical causes harmful algal blooms.

POLLUTION

Pollution is a major problem in many wetlands, and it takes many forms. Road salt and waste oil drain into wetlands from streets and parking lots, weakening or killing plants and animals. Harmful substances in farm runoff, smokestack **emissions,** and wastewater discharges build up in wetlands. In less developed countries, untreated or improperly treated **sewage** contaminates wetlands.

Eutrophication

One of the most common results of wetland pollution is a condition called **eutrophication.** In this condition, water quality gradually gets worse, and the wetland becomes unable to support much, if any, animal life. Eutrophication typically begins when nitrates and phosphates—chemicals in **fertilizers,** detergents, animal wastes, and improperly treated sewage—enter a wetland. These chemicals serve as nutrients for algae, which then begin to reproduce more frequently. As more and more of these chemicals enter the wetland, thick layers of algae—called **algal blooms**—spread across the water surface.

After algae in the lower, older layers of the blooms die, bacteria decompose the dead algae. Bacteria use oxygen in the water as they carry out decomposition. When large amounts of algae are being broken down by bacteria, the oxygen supply in a wetland decreases. Fish and other water-living animals need the oxygen in the water to live, and so they begin to die in greater numbers. Their bodies then provide more organic material for bacterial decomposition, which uses up even more oxygen. Eventually, there may not be enough oxygen left in the water for any life to survive.

Eutrophication sometimes leads to an entire wetland disappearing. This happens when the organic waste builds up to the point that the wetland becomes completely filled in. Then, grasses, weeds, shrubs, and trees take root in the area of the former wetland. Eutrophication happens naturally over thousands of years. However, pollution has caused eutrophication to occur much faster in many wetlands.

Other pollutants

Wetland pollution can harm the health of humans. Toxic substances, including such metals as arsenic, lead, and mercury, may enter ground water supplies through wetlands. These substances may cause illness if the ground water is used as a source of drinking water. Animal and human wastes contaminate some wetlands that are used as sources of drinking water—especially in less developed countries. Contaminated drinking water causes such illnesses as cholera, dysentery, and typhoid fever.

In the United States, the Clean Water Act **regulates** the discharge of untreated water and harmful chemicals into wetlands and other bodies of water. Other industrialized nations have similar laws and regulations. Such legislation has reduced pollution from most **point sources**, which are easily identifiable sources of pollutants, such as smokestack emissions and wastewater discharges. Unfortunately, water pollution from nonpoint sources, such as runoff from construction sites and farmland, remains mostly uncontrolled. Furthermore, many less developed countries have no effective water treatment processes for preventing pollutants from contaminating wetlands.

GREEN FACT

A large region low in oxygen and with few living organisms forms each spring and summer in the Gulf of Mexico. This **"dead zone"** forms as waters emptied into the gulf by the Mississippi River deposit agricultural pollutants that cause eutrophication. This area of depleted oxygen sometimes grows to the size of New Jersey. There are many other dead zones throughout the world.

Fertilizers and other wastes promote algae growth. Such algal blooms use up oxygen in water.

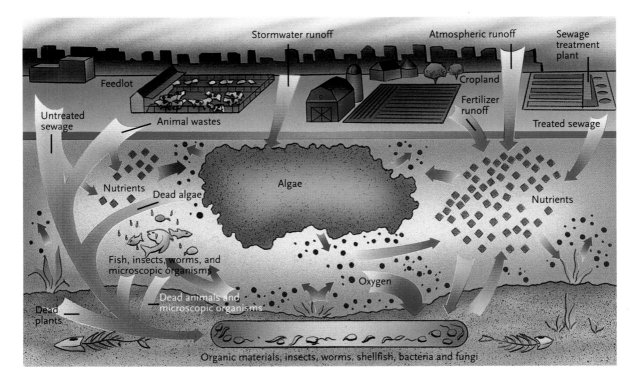

INVASIVE SPECIES

The plants and animals that occur naturally in any wetland evolved in their habitats with factors that place limits on their populations. For example, species compete with each other for food and shelter. This competition prevents any one species from becoming too numerous at the expense of others. Naturally occurring insect pests and diseases also limit plant and animal populations—as do local weather conditions.

An invasive plant species called hydrilla chokes the surface of a canal in Florida's Everglades.

Such factors place limits on the populations of organisms when the organisms and factors develop together over hundreds of thousands of years. These limits provide a natural ecological balance to a wetland. However, this balance can become upset when an organism from a different environment is introduced to a wetland by humans. The introduced organism finds itself in a new place in which there are no natural limits or controls to its population growth—including no natural predators, parasites, or diseases. Such an organism may be able to reproduce and spread throughout a region unchecked. Such introduced species—also called **invasive species** or exotic species—have caused ecological damage to many wetlands.

Examples of invasive species

At least 100 invasive species of plants have spread across the Everglades in southern Florida. The Brazilian pepper tree was introduced into the Everglades as an ornamental tree in the mid-1800's. It has since scattered across thousands of square miles. People purposefully introduced the water-sucking tree to the Everglades to help dry up the land. These trees now form dense, widespread **monocultures**. Hydrilla and water hyacinth (*HY uh sihnth*), aquarium plants released into the Everglades, have filled up many watery areas at the expense of native plants.

Many exotic animal species have also been introduced into various wetlands, causing population declines in native species. Among such animals are certain species of clams, mussels, snails, crayfish, crabs, insects, fish, frogs, snakes, lizards, birds, and rodents.

Controlling invasive species

In some cases, people purposefully release exotic species into new areas, not realizing the damage they will cause. In other cases, the releases are accidental. Seeds from nursery or garden plants are sometimes carried to a wetland by birds or wind. Immature shellfish sometimes arrive in a coastal area when a ship dumps its ballast water (water taken on at sea for balance). Pet pythons have been released into the Everglades, where they have quickly spread and threaten native wildlife.

Once established in a natural area, an invasive species can be virtually impossible to eliminate. Wetland managers usually seek to merely control the spread of the foreign species. This goal can be accomplished in a number of ways. Specially made **herbicides** may be used to kill only selected plant species. People may also try to remove harmful plant species by cutting, burning, and flooding. Insects from the native regions of exotic animal species may be used as parasites or predators to kill the invaders.

Invasive zebra mussels were first introduced to the United States in 1988.

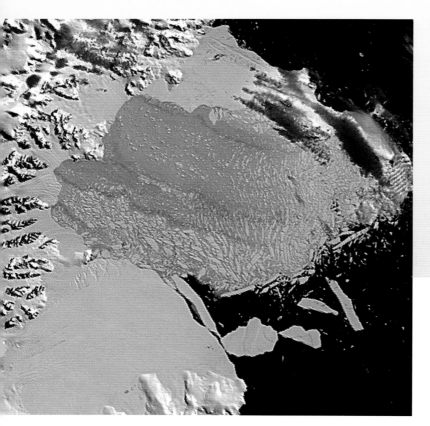

Melting polar ice can raise the sea level, flooding wetlands. This Antarctic ice shelf collapsed in 2002.

CLIMATE CHANGE

Scientists expect that a warming climate will have serious effects on wetland ecosystems. These effects are likely to vary, depending on the region in which the wetland lies. Plant and animal species may shift their ranges to new areas. The water quality of wetlands may deteriorate. Some wetlands may dry up, while others may be exposed to flooding.

Shifting animals

Scientists with the Pew Center on Global Climate Change, a research institute in Arlington, Virginia, have predicted that **global warming** may cause animal species adapted to cooler weather, such as trout and salmon, to disappear from much of their current range. By contrast, species adapted to warmer weather, such as bass and carp, may expand their ranges.

Climate-related changes in animal behavior have already been observed with some wetland birds, including certain species of kingfishers, plovers, and sandpipers. These birds now undertake their annual spring migrations earlier in the year than they did in the mid-1900's. Many scientists believe that these changes were triggered by warmer weather occurring earlier in the year.

Water quality

The water quality of many wetlands may decline as a result of higher temperatures and drier conditions. Higher temperatures typically lead to faster growth of algal blooms, which cause reduced oxygen levels and eutrophication of wetlands. In some wetlands, less rainfall will lead to reductions in the runoff of nutrient-rich surface water into the wetlands. These wetlands may then not get enough nutrients to maintain a healthy ecosystem, leading to the deaths of plants and animals.

Drying and flooding

Many meteorologists believe that global warming is altering precipitation patterns around the world. Although these changes may cause wetlands in some regions to dry up, wetlands in other regions could be harmed by flooding.

Damage from flooding would be most severe in coastal wetlands, such as salt marshes and mangrove swamps. According to some computer models, sea levels could rise several feet or meters if ice sheets on Antarctica and Greenland melt into the ocean. Researchers with the United Nations' Intergovernmental Panel on Climate Change have reported that the average sea level around the world has already risen by more than 4 inches (10 centimeters) since the early 1900's. They attributed this rise mostly to thermal expansion—that is, warmer water taking up more volume than cooler water. As sea levels continue to rise, wetlands along seacoasts could disappear into the sea.

It is impossible to know for sure how particular wetlands will be affected by continued global warming. Nevertheless, actions can be taken to reduce the risks of ecological damage. Reductions in emissions of **carbon dioxide** and other **greenhouse gases** are crucial to slowing global warming.

A tsunami destroyed this Sri Lankan bus station in 2004. Tsunamis can devastate coastal environments, such as wetlands.

A CLOSER LOOK
Climate Models

A climate computer model is based on mathematical equations about sunlight, heat, rainfall, wind, ocean currents, and other factors. Scientists change these equations in different ways to simulate the ways that these factors might change in the real world. The computer model then outputs the most likely effects that these factors would have on Earth's climate.

In the early 2000's, a group of climate experts created three simulations to determine the cause of global warming over the past 100 years. Each simulation measured the temperature of Earth based on a set of factors. The first simulation included both natural processes and human activities. The second simulation included only natural processes, while the third included only human activities. The scientists then compared these results with actual temperatures. The first model proved to be the most accurate. Based on these results, the climate experts concluded that human activities are the main cause of global warming.

Activities

ORGANIZE A CLEANUP DAY

Introduction

Protecting animal **habitats** and the environment can begin right in your community. Together with family and friends, you can organize a cleanup day in nearby local parks, beaches, or nature preserves.

Materials:

- Garbage bags
- Rubber gloves
- Poster board
- Markers
- A group of family, friends, and community members

Directions:

1. Once you have chosen a day to hold the event, create posters that give information about your cleanup day. Include details such as the day, place, time, and reason for the event. Get permission to hang these posters at school and at local businesses. You may also want to include a "rain date" in case weather prevents your cleanup day from taking place.
2. On the day of the event, distribute garbage bags and gloves to volunteers, and assign areas for people to cover. When the event is over, you can take the collected garbage to a waste center in your town.
3. Keeping Earth clean is a continuous process. Be sure to hold cleanup days regularly in your community!

RESEARCH PROJECT: FORESTS AND WETLANDS OF THE WORLD

Introduction

Earth is home to a fascinating variety of forests and wetlands. Each has its own unique ecosystem with an amazing number of plant and animal species. You can learn more about these habitats by researching them at your library.

Directions:

1. Choose a forest or wetland habitat you wish to learn more
   about. You can choose your own or one from the lists below:

Forests

Amazon rain forest
Andean tropical rain forests and cloud forests
Central American cloud forests
Colombian rain forests
Caribbean tropical forests
East African tropical forests
Hawaiian tropical rain forest
Himalayan forests
Indonesian rain forests
Madagascar tropical rain forest
North American temperate rain forests
Philippine rain forests
South American temperate rain forests
The taiga
West African tropical rain forests

Wetlands

Arctic tundra
Danube river delta, Europe
Ganges-Brahmaputra River
Huang He, China
Indus River
Florida Everglades, United States
Florida mangrove swamps, United States
McKenzie River, Canada
Mississippi River, United States
Niger River, Africa
Nile River, Africa
Oak Hammock Marsh, Manitoba, Canada
Pripet marshes, Northern Europe
Volga River delta, Europe
Yukon River, North America

2. Ask your teacher or school or public librarian to help you find information on the region you chose to research. Together, come up with a
   list of things you'd like to find out about this area. Examples of such
   questions include:

- What makes this region unique?
- What is the climate in this region?
- What plants and animals live here?
- What plants and animals used to live here?
- How has this habitat changed in recent years?
- What are the largest threats to this habitat today?
- How are people working to protect this habitat?

3. Create a report that gives important information about the habitat.
   The report could be in the form of a booklet, poster, collage, blog,
   podcast, or a combination of media.

Glossary

acid rain rain that has a high concentration of acids because of air pollution.

adaptation a trait that helps an organism survive in its natural environment.

algal bloom a sudden, abnormal explosion of the population of algae in a body of water caused by large amounts of nutrients in the water.

biodiversity the amount of variety among plants, animals, and other organisms.

biome a natural community of plants and animals in a region, mostly determined by climate.

by-product an additional product created in the manufacture of an object or substance.

canopy the top layer of tree growth in a rain forest.

carbon dioxide a colorless, odorless gas given off by burning and by animals breathing out.

carnivore an animal that feeds chiefly on flesh; a plant that digests insects.

chemical warfare the use of gases, flames, smoke, or any chemical other than explosives as weapons.

chloroplast a structure in plant cells that carries out photosynthesis.

clearcutting the removal of all the trees in a certain area of forest.

conifer a tree that bears its seeds in cones.

conservation the management, protection, and wise use of natural resources.

consumer an animal that eats plants or other animals.

dead zone an area in the ocean with too little oxygen for plant and animal life to survive.

deciduous refers to trees or shrubs that shed their leaves at a certain time of year.

decomposer a bacteria, fungus, or other organism that breaks down the remains of other organisms.

decompose to break down; decay.

deforestation the destruction of forests.

degradation damage caused to a natural area as a result of pollution or other factors.

dormancy the condition of being inactive.

ecological succession the gradual development of a forest or other natural area through a series of changes in the kinds of plants and animals that live in the area.

ecosystem a group of interrelated living things and the environment on which they depend.

emergent a tall tree in a tropical rain forest that rises above the layer of the canopy; a plant that grows from the bottom of a wetland to above the water surface.

emission an airborne waste product.

epiphyte a plant that grows on another plant for support but manufactures its own food through photosynthesis.

estivation the period of inactivity when environmental conditions are hot or dry.

ethanol a widely used biofuel made from plants or algae; ethyl alcohol.

eutrophication the build-up of excessive nutrients in a body of water, causing rapid growth of algae and depletion of oxygen.

evaporate to change from a liquid or solid into a vapor or gas.

fertilizer a substance that helps plants to grow.

foliage the leaves of a plant.

fossil fuel underground deposits that were formed millions of years ago from the remains of plants and animals. Coal, oil, and natural gas are fossil fuels.

global warming the gradual warming of Earth's surface, believed to be caused by a build-up of greenhouse gases in the atmosphere.

greenhouse gas any gas that contributes to the greenhouse effect.

greenhouse effect the process by which certain gases cause the Earth's atmosphere to warm.

ground water water that pools underground in porous rocks.

guerrillas a band of fighters who conduct such activities as sudden raids, ambushes, and disruption of supply lines against government forces.

habitat the place where an animal or plant naturally lives or grows.

herbicide a poison that kills weeds.

herbivore an animal that feeds on plants.

invasive species a living thing that is transported to a new environment where it spreads rapidly and threatens local wildlife.

invertebrate an animal without a backbone.

Kyoto Protocol the international agreement that set limits for the amount of greenhouse gases that countries can produce.

larvae the early, immature stage in the growth of an insect.

monoculture the growth of only one kind of crop.

monsoon a wind that changes direction with the season (especially in southern Asia), causing heavy rains in one season and drought in another season.

mutualism a relationship between two species of living things in which both benefit.

omnivore an animal that eats both plants and animals.

ozone a form of oxygen gas.

peat a spongy substance made of partially decayed plant material.

permafrost permanently frozen soil.

pesticide a poison that kills pests, such as insects.

pH scale the scale used to assess the degree of acidity or alkalinity of a solution, ranging from 0 (very acidic) to 14 (very alkaline).

photosynthesis the process by which plant cells make energy from sunlight.

pollutant a single source of pollution.

point source an identified source of pollution.

precipitation rain, snow, sleet, ice, or hail.

producer a plant or alga that produces food through photosynthesis.

raptor a bird of prey, such as a hawk.

refugee a person who flees war, disaster, or other problems for safety.

regulate; regulation to control by rule, principle, or system.

relative humidity the ratio between the amount of water vapor in the air and the greatest amount of water vapor that the air could contain.

scrubber an air pollution control system that filters out harmful pollutants from emissions in power plants and factories.

sewage water that contains waste matter produced by human beings.

slash-and-burn agriculture cutting down and burning forests to prepare the land for farming.

smog a brown, hazy mixture of gases and particulates caused by exhaust gases released by automobiles and other users of fossil fuels.

strata layers of vegetation in a forest, such as the layers of tall trees, shrubs, and ground-level plants.

subcanopy a layer of trees just below the canopy in a rain forest.

submergent a plant that remains mostly or completely underwater.

sustainable any practice that adheres to principles of conservation and ecological balance.

temperate not very hot, and not very cold.

transpiration the release of water vapor through the stomata (pores) of a leaf.

tundra cold, dry, treeless lands of the Arctic.

ultraviolet rays the invisible rays in the part of the spectrum beyond the violet.

understory the low layer of plants forming an underbrush or underwood.

United Nations an international organization that works for world peace and human prosperity.

Additional Resources

WEB SITES

Canadian Environmental Assessment Agency

http://www.ceaa-acee.gc.ca

Provides environmental assessments that contribute to well-informed decision making; supports sustainable development.

Environment Agency

http://www.environment-agency.gov.uk

Provides tools to make the environment a better place for you and for future generations; includes resources for schools.

International Union for Conservation of Nature

http://cms.iucn.org/

Works to find practical solutions to environmental and development challenges.

National Geographic

http://www.nationalgeographic.com/

Features articles, video, and photography of environmental issues around the world; includes a student section with games and activities.

Natural Resources Defense Council

http://www.nrdc.org/

Contains the latest information on ways people are working toward environmentally friendly practices.

The Nature Conservancy

http://www.nature.org

Works to protect ecologically important lands and waters; includes an activities section.

Rainforest Conservation Fund

http://www.rainforestconservation.org/

Works to ensure the future of tropical rain forests.

United States Environmental Protection Agency

http://www.epa.gov

Many directions to go from homepage for information on the environment, including a student page

World Wildlife Fund

http://www.worldwildlife.org/

An organization that helps protect animals and ecosystems around the world.

BOOKS

Animal Survivors of the Wetlands
by Barbara A. Somervill (Scholastic Publishing, 2004)

Disappearing Forests
by Angela Royston (Heinemann Library, 2008)

The Down-to-Earth Guide to Global Warming
by Laurie David and Cambria Gordon (Orchard Books, 2007)

Encyclopedia of Global Environmental Change
(John Wiley & Sons Ltd, 2002)

Endangered Planet
by David Burnie and Tony Juniper (Kingfisher, 2007)

Index

A

acacia trees, 28

acid rain, 34

adaptation, 11

Africa, 29, 37

Agent Orange, 36

agriculture, 32-33

algal blooms, 52, 53, 56

animals, forest, 4-7; boreal forests, 21; global warming and, 38-39; poaching of, 37; temperate forests, 11, 13, 17; tropical forests, 25, 29

animals, wetland, 4-5, 40-43; bogs and fens, 48-49; Everglades, 50, 51; global warming and, 56; invasive species, 54-55; marshes, 44-45; swamps, 47

ants, 28

Army Corps of Engineers, U.S., 51

B

bacteria, 42, 48, 52

baldcypress trees, 46

baobab trees, 26

beetles, bark, 38-39

biodiversity, 22, 32

biomass, 16

biomes, 6

birds, 5; forest, 13, 17, 21, 25, 29; wetland, 41, 45, 47-49, 56

bogs, 5, 41, 42, 48-49

Brazil, 33

broadleaf trees, 7, 12, 16, 24

butterflies, 42

C

canopy, of forest, 4, 24, 28

capybaras, 25, 45

carbon dioxide, 8, 23; in global warming, 38, 39, 57

carnivores, 8

carnivorous plants, 48

catalytic converters, 35

chemical warfare, 36

chlorophyll, 7, 12

Clean Air Act, 35

cleanup day, 58

Clean Water Act, 35, 53

clearcutting, 30

climate, 5, 23; computer models, 57. *See also* global warming *and specfic habitats*

conifers, 12, 14-20, 46

conservation, 31, 33, 37, 51

Conservation International, 33

consumers (organisms), 8, 42

cougars, 17

cypress trees, 46

D

dead zones, 53

deciduous trees, 7. *See also* forests

decomposition, 8, 42

deforestation, 30

desnudo trees, 28

dormancy, 12

dormice, 13

duckweed, 43

E

ecological succession, 9

ecosystems: forest, 7-9, 30-31, 36; wetland, 42-43, 56

emergents (plants), 24, 42

epiphytes, 16, 24, 46

erosion, 43

estivation, 29

ethanol, 33

eutrophication, 52, 56

Everglades, 50-51, 54, 55

evergreen trees, 7, 14-20

F

farming, 32-33

fens, 41, 48-49

fir trees, 16, 20

fish, 25, 45, 49, 52

flooding, 43, 57

floor, of forest, 24

food chain, 8, 42

forests, 4-7; boreal, 18-21, 38-39, 39; ecology, 8-9; farming and, 32-33; global warming and, 38-39; logging and, 30-31; mixed deciduous-evergreen, 14-15; montane, 14-16; old-growth, 9; projects, 58-59; temperate coniferous, 14-17; temperate deciduous, 10-13, 39; tropical seasonal, 26-29; warfare and, 36-37. *See also* rain forests; swamps

Forest Service, U.S., 31

fossil fuels, 23, 35

G

General Sherman Tree, 17

global warming, 23, 38-39, 56-57

greenhouse effect, 23, 38, 39

ground water, 9, 40, 53

guerrilla warfare, 36

Gulf of Mexico, 53

gumbo-limbo trees, 28

H

herbicides, 36, 55

herbivores, 8, 13

herons, 47
hibernation, 13, 29
hydrilla plants, 54, 55

I

ice, polar, 56, 57
India, 29
insects: forest, 13, 21, 25, 38-39;
  wetland, 45, 48-49
Intergovernmental Panel on Climate Change (IPCC), 38, 39, 57
invasive species, 54-55

J

Japan, 36

K

Kyoto Protocol, 39

L

larches, 20
leaves, falling, 7, 12
lemurs, 29
logging, 30-31
Long-Range Transboundary Air Pollution Agreement, 35
lynxes, 13, 21

M

mammals: forest, 13, 17, 21, 25, 29;
  wetland, 45, 49
mangrove trees, 46, 47
maple trees, 12, 46
marshes, 5, 41, 44-45
martens, 17
monkeys, 8
monocultures, 32-33, 54
monsoons, 26-27, 29
moss, 48
mummies, 5
mussels, zebra, 55
mutualism, 28

O

omnivores, 8

owls, 7
oxbow lakes, 46
ozone, 34, 35

P

panthers, Florida, 51
peat, 41, 48
permafrost, 19
pesticides, 34, 50
Pew Center on Global Climate Change, 56
photosynthesis, 8, 9, 15, 34, 39, 42
pines, 16-17, 19
pitcher plants, 48
plants, forest, 4-7; boreal forests,
  20-21; global warming and, 38;
  temperate forests, 11-13, 16-17;
  tropical forests, 24, 28
plants, wetland, 41-43; bogs and
  fens, 48, 49; Everglades, 50, 51;
  invasive species, 54-55;
  marshes, 45; swamps, 46-47
playa lakes, 44, 45
pneumatophores, 46
poaching, 37
pollution, 34-35, 43, 52-53
prairie potholes, 44
producers (organisms), 8, 42

R

rafflesia flowers, 25
rain, 7, 23, 34
rain forests: temperate, 14; tropical, 7-9, 22-25, 27, 33, 37
Ramsar Convention on Wetlands,
  51
ranching, 32-33
redwoods, 16
refugees, 37
Rio Declaration, 37
runoff, 31, 34-35, 43, 56
Rwanda, 37

S

salamanders, 17
scrubbers, 35
sea level, 50, 57
sequoias, 16, 17
sinkholes, 45
skunk cabbage, 11
slash-and-burn agriculture, 32
smog, 34, 35
soybeans, 33
spills, chemical, 33-34
squirrels, 21
subcanopy, of forest, 24
submergents (plants), 42, 45
swamps, 5, 41, 46-47

T

timber line, 19
topsoil, 31
transpiration, 23
trees. See forests and specific types
tsunamis, 57
tundra, 6, 18, 40

U

understory, of forest, 24
United Nations (UN), 37-39, 57

V

vernal pools, 44
Vietnam War, 36

W

warfare, 36-37
water lilies, 42
water moccasins, 47
wetlands, 4-5, 21, 40; ecology, 42-43; global warming and, 56-57;
  human settlement of, 50-51; invasive species, 54-55; location
  of, 40-41; pollution, 52-53; projects, 58-59. See also specific types
woodchucks, 13